Financial Globalization and Post-Communist Georgia

Financial Globalization and Post-Communist Georgia

✦

Global Exchange Rate Instability and its Implications for Georgia

Vladimer Papava
and
Vepkhia Chocheli

iUniverse, Inc.
New York Lincoln Shanghai

Financial Globalization and Post-Communist Georgia
Global Exchange Rate Instability and its Implications for Georgia

iUniverse, Inc.

For information address:
iUniverse, Inc.
2021 Pine Lake Road, Suite 100
Lincoln, NE 68512
www.iuniverse.com

ISBN: 0-595-30043-X

Printed in the United States of America

Contents

Introduction

The prominent Austrian economist, Joseph Schumpeter, labeled capitalism as a system of "constructive destruction". He explained this by the quality of new goods, innovative technologies and ideas to force uncompetitive goods and out-dated technologies and ideas out of market. Such replacements promote the country's advancement and, at the same time, cause the destruction of the old system.

Relative to market economy, the Socialist system was the complete opposite of it. It might be labeled as a system of "conserved non-construction". Although production kept growing, it was of no actual benefit to the public.

At the same time, one can not overlook the fact that during the transition to market economy (the positive impact of which in a long-term perspective can not be questioned) many forms of economic activities lost competitive qualities, which fact, in part, is a result of the growing economic and financial globaliza-tion. If you add to this the collapse of external economic relationships between the countries of the former Socialist bloc, resulting in the significant fall of exports, the reasons behind such a deep economic crisis will become more than apparent.

Over the last couple of years, dozens of countries embarked on comprehensive reforms oriented towards democracy and market economy. The key idea on which all of those reforms were based was that the country's prosperity and improvement of living standard could only be achieved if a healthy market eco-nomic system, closely integrated with the global economy, would be established.

Only today one could state with sufficient confidence that a universal consen-sus in favor of market economy has almost been achieved. Furthermore, when-ever market is coupled with a social security system, it becomes possible to recover–if not completely, at least partially–social costs of the market-based sys-tem.

Obviously, the collapse of the Communist regime across the world, on the one hand, and the expansion of the coverage area of market-based system (which, *inter alia*, has incorporated the huge majority of post-Communist countries) (see, for example, Stroev, Bliakhman, Krotov, 1999), on the other hand, significantly improved the "quality" of economic and financial globalization (see, for example, Rumer, 2000).

At the same time, transformation of "closed" economies into "open" ones, closely integrated with international highly competitive commodity, currency and financial markets, on the one hand, increased the likelihood of economy's exposure to external economic shocks, on the other hand, however, enabled maximization of the effective use of economic resources (see, for example, Dornbush (ed.), 1993).

Under such circumstances, almost in all cases, economic developments taking place in any particular country may have an increasingly powerful impact on the global economy, especially as the world's financial system is based on electronic links and the dissemination and exchange of information, as a factor of production, takes place in an automatic mode.

Although there is a multitude of scientific and analytic literature on the problem of economic and financial globalization, a major set of issues still have to be discussed, whereas certain, the most sophisticated practical or theoretical problems have not been solved yet. Along with many good things that globalization brings about, it causes some serious problems (see, for example, Ellwood, 2001; Stiglitz, 2002), and particularly to small countries (see, for example, Rondeli, 2003), not all of which can be solved in a short period of time (see, for example, Zhukow, 2000).

At the same time, it must be noted that in most cases the problems caused by globalization are identical in various countries, which is why it is especially important to develop some standard solutions. Nevertheless, it is also doubtless that economic "recipes" for "small" and "big" countries can be different and it would be a mistake to apply only a uniform approach to all of them (see, for example, Connoly, de Melo (ed.), 1994).

The present book consists of four chapters. We would like to draw reader's attention to several–very important from our point of view–aspects which are discussed in detail below.

The book starts with discussions on Georgia's international economic function, i.e. the role that Georgia plays in the global economy. Focus is made on specific characteristics of monetary policy under the conditions of post-Communist transformation of economy. Further, inflation's impact on economic growth is reviewed and based on a Georgian example is argued that under the conditions of transition to market a high inflation rate can not promote economic growth.

The book also evaluates an international monetary and financial system development potential in the context of "corporate crises" started in the USA in late 2001 and a probable impact of the latter on international financial markets, on the one hand, and changing international business activities, on the other hand.

In this connection, two quite sensational forecasts made during the last two years regarding the collapse of the US Dollar are analyzed. These forecasts make a pretty "gloomy picture" of the future of both the US Dollar and the international monetary system. It is argued that such a scenario is not likely to occur.

It is further maintained that with the introduction of a common European currency, the Euro, a "new three-pole world currency system" was established on the strength of which will depend, a good deal, the stability of global economy.

The substance of a "new economy" (see, for example, Kelly, 1998) is explored and it is argued that it is not fair to suppose that growing disproportion between the "new" (informational) and the "old" (traditional) sectors of economy is responsible for international economic crisis, as under the conditions "of new economy", the improved management of the streams of information and–owing to new technologies–the more efficient disposition of stocks enabled a more efficient use of economic resources which, coupled with the increased productivity and the greater competition, will keep inflation under control.

Also, one must take into account the "shortcomings" of financial accounting and standards which can satisfy the requirements of "new economy" just in part. To some extent, those are responsible for the spread of "corporate crisis" too.

It is demonstrated that as a small economy, Georgia cannot have any substantial influence on global economic developments; however, if it succeeds to pursue more-or-less reasonable economic policy, it may generate some positive results, not to mention the minimization of clearly negative ones.

Because of complexity of the problem, we almost completely realize that some readers may not agree to the views expressed by the authors in this book. We would be pleased to accept any constructive critical remarks.

1

Georgia's Role and Function in the World Economy

1.1. Georgia's Independence and the Danger of Revenge

Georgia is a country of 4.3 million covering 70.000 square kilometers and bordered by Russia, Azerbaijan, Armenia, Turkey and the Black Sea. The country has traditionally served as an important trade and transit corridor between Europe and Asia.

Georgia was among the first republics of the Former Soviet Union (FSU) to declare independence doing so April 9, 1991 (Metreveli, 1995). Although official pre-independence statistics on per capita income ranked Georgia relatively low among the republics of the FSU, it was in fact relatively well-off due in part to a strong tradition of entrepreneurship and an agricultural sector with significant private sector activity.

Existence of the FSU depended on extensive use of rich natural resources. The country's industrial development though was based on a hard compulsory labor of the immense and cheap workforce living under the State's severe oppression. In the meantime, economic strength of the nation, a good deal, was dependent on the world prices of oil and other natural resources, the fluctuation of which would accordingly result in an increase or cut of the country's hard currency revenues. As a potential of extensive use of natural resources is objectively limited, it was obvious that from the standpoint of its economic base the Soviet system was essentially unpromising. If you add to this the FSU's involvement in the Cold War during many decades–which actually was an inadmissible luxury for the country–it will become clear that the accelerated breakdown of the Soviet empire was an inevitable result from both the inner economic problems and the outside political pressure on the FSU. The striving of some former Soviet republics, including Georgia (Gachechiladze, 1995), for the reestablishment of national independence was an additional factor pushing up this fatal process.

As of the present, Georgia has still not fully conceived its economic policy and essentially has no strategic vision of its development. The occasional debates about which area it should focus on—agrarian or industrial, or which function in general each of its branches should carry out—can hardly be considered constructive. After all, every state at each historical stage of its existence has to resolve a set of problems regarding its economic development, the most important being the choice of a reliable strategy of progress, on the basis of which practical measures are also determined. This problem is particularly urgent for Georgia today, the leadership of which, since the latest restoration of the state's independence (the beginning of the 1990s), has mainly been engaged in resolving what are of course important tactical tasks, but are in no way related to the development of strategy. So it goes without saying that Georgia's place and role, as well as its function in the world economy, must be comprehended at the proper level.

With respect to general acceptance of the idea of state independence, the period beginning after 9 April, 1989, when Moscow conducted a punitive campaign against the peaceful residents of Tbilisi, can be considered a revolutionary turning point in the mindset of the country's population. It goes without saying that this also had an impact on the economic mindset. At that time, a number of noteworthy *romantic* conceptions appeared regarding the republic's economic independence (Papava, 1991). In some of them, the solutions to several problems were expressed rather vaguely.

Despite these objective shortcomings, on the basis of the conceptions mentioned, the strategic contours of Georgia's economy took shape: its independence (which is identified with independence from Russia) based on a market system (although even the outlines of this system were not defined). At that time, this seemed entirely sufficient to begin political reforms, reject the communist-oriented economy, and approve the institution of private property.

But after the peaceful (on the basis of elections) overturn of the communist regime, the romantic idea of state independence assumed a very *extremist* form: the striving to achieve independence from Russia as quickly as possible became extremely urgent, and transformation of the economy was postponed for the indefinite future.

Any extremism is destructive. And, naturally, any fight for independence taken to the extreme (the most graphic example of this is 1991 when Georgia closed its railroad in order to set up a supposedly economic blockade against Russia) cannot yield good results: the administrative management system was not replaced by a market system, but on the other hand all ties with enterprises of the former Soviet expanse were hastily and mechanically destroyed.

The country and its economy were not in an extreme state for long. This was particularly due to the fact that the difficulties associated with the forced change in power (the winter of 1991-1992) and accompanied by military action in South Ossetia and Abkhazia, and corruption of the state management apparatus, along with a torrent of errors in economic policy (credit and budget emission resulted in hyperinflation (Gurgenidze, Lobzhanidze, Onoprishvili, 1994), led to a four-fold drop in production (Papava, 1995; Papava, Beridze, 1994). The complicated social problems (Papava, Chikovani (ed.), 1997) that arose in this connection dampened the extremist tendencies.

But at the same time, a thirst for *political revenge* was manifested in some members of government for the first time. In particular, the parliament speaker cast doubts on the expediency of the existence of an independent Georgian state, and the ability of the Georgians to independently govern the country. Based on this, he demanded that the republic be incorporated into the "ruble zone" (admittedly, the IMF also upheld a similar view, which was subsequently recognized as its big mistake (Åslund, 1995, ch., 4; Lavigne, 1995, p. 207)). This essentially meant rejecting economic independence. If the country's authorities had gone this route, the country would have been under Russia's influence again. To be fair, it should be noted that if the republic's leadership had supported the proposal put forward in 1993 by the leaders of revenge to return the country to the "ruble zone," Russia would probably not have accepted us, since at that point, it was not ready itself for this development in events, as least economically. What is more, an unstable, criminal, and hyperinflated country could not be considered ready for joining this zone.

The stance of the economic avengers was shaken somewhat in 1994 when the anti-crisis program of macroeconomic stabilization was launched, and faltered even more when monetary reform was successfully completed in 1995 (Papava, 1996, 1998, 1999; Papava, Beridze, 1998; Wang, 1998; Wellisz, 1996). The Constitution adopted and the presidential and parliamentary elections conducted dealt the avengers even harsher blows.

And although today the idea of a "ruble zone" can be called dead (or at least "slumbering"), the avengers' plans and scope of action have not only failed to shrink, but are gaining greater momentum.

The budget crisis and increase in corruption (Gotsiridze, Kandelaki, 2001; Papava, 2000B) that began in 1998 dramatically aggravated the population's social position, for which the avengers blamed those in favor of a market economy. And this is creating the possibility of *social revenge*; for example, the advocators of nationalization and de-privatization of property are making themselves heard with increasing frequency, which is supported by corrupt politicians striving for cheap popularity. There is the real danger that the fight against corruption will escalate into social revenge.

Present-day Georgia is in a state where the government's mistakes (Gotsiridze, Kandelaki, 2001; Papava, 2002A) are making it easy for the supporters of a return to the past to increase pressure on the authorities and force them to approve the Russian orientation in the country's strategic development vision. On its part, Russia is ready for reintegration processes, the best example being its unification with Belarus, although it should be noted that the positive economic benefit from this union is unconvincing to say the least.

Not only virulent communists, but also political forces (consciously or unconsciously), camouflaged as patriots, laborites, and socialists, and who by their very nature have the same communist mentality, are "working" on the idea of revenge. They are no longer satisfied with the idea of joining the "ruble zone," they are striving, as already noted, to annul privatization, restore social pseudo-guarantees, and ultimately turn back the wheels of history.

Consequently, at the current stage, the revenge approach to the vision of the country's economic (and not only economic) development is gaining momentum, based on reintegrating ties with Russia, complete isolation from Europe, destruction of the private property institution (at best only allowing small businesses), restoring the directive principles of a planned economy, and so on.

Of course, the question arises of whether there is an alternative to the revenge strategy, and if so, what.

1.2. Georgia's Economic Attraction

It can be said that Georgia has always striven to become not only a geographic part of Europe. But during the past centuries, this striving was one-sided, and unfortunately its cherished wish did not come true.

Fortunately, during the first years of state independence restoration (1991-1993), its pull toward Europe manifested itself again, but the voice of the supporters of this trend could not always be heard against the chaos instigated by the extremists and then the avengers.

Georgia has been a member of the Council of Europe since 1999, and in so doing, the country's western orientation has been recognized at an international level. This is clearly a major achievement, although it does not mean that Georgia is already an inviolable part of integrated Europe, since this requires becoming a member of the European Union and NATO (Rondeli, 2001).

Desire alone is not enough to become an intrinsic part of Europe, it is only a necessary condition which also requires Europe's desire to recognize Georgia as its fundamental part. And this is based on at least two conditions: first, Georgia must correspond to the standards of democracy, protection of human rights, and level of economic development recognized in the West, and second, our country joining this union must also be economically advantageous to Europe.

How can Georgia's economy attract Europe and the rest of the world? Unfortunately, even theoretically the market not only of Georgia, but also of the entire Southern Caucasus, is so small (due to the territory Georgia has temporarily lost and the military opposition between Azerbaijan and Armenia) that there is absolutely no need to invest in improving and developing its production in order to satisfy the country's current consumer and production demand. This demand can be satisfied by means of import, which is confirmed by the practice of recent years, when strategic investors (apart from those party to pipeline projects) came to Georgia mainly to acquaint themselves with the situation (and not for real activity), and actual investments were carried out by relatively small companies (not to mention the dubious origin and goals of some of them). If we also take into account our direct neighbors, Russia and Turkey, it becomes utterly clear that Georgia's demand, as well as that of the Southern Caucasus as a whole, can be satisfied primarily by import from these countries. Consequently, Georgia, from the viewpoint of meeting its consumer and production demand, cannot be of any interest to Europe, not to mention the rest of the world (Papava, Gogatadze, 1998).

The solution to this seemingly hopeless situation should be sought in Georgia's *international economic function* as an independent state (Papava, 2002C). It should be stressed that in the modern world each country has a specific function and its level of economic development and role in the world integration process is determined by the extent to which it is in harmony with the international economic functions of other states.

1.3. From Europe and to Asia

In international relations (including economic), two systems, which are already classical, have developed today: "East-West" and "North-South." It is believed that economically and from the point of view of democratic institutions, the West is more developed than the East. Naturally, this idea is provisional, as is most graphically shown by Japan, China, and South Korea, which surpass many western countries in terms of economic development. The "North-South" system is even more provisional, since the US, Canada, and the Northern European states are more developed (both economically and politically) than those countries located to the south of them. But this situation in no way applies to relatively backward Russia.

In order to reveal Georgia's international economic function, its place must be determined in the "East-West" and "North-South" systems.

Whereas the "West" as a whole, as mentioned above, can be viewed as economically more developed than the "East," the latter is rich in natural resources. Naturally, based on the need to balance supply and demand (according to the principles of an open market economy), the need arises to activate bilateral transportation flows in the "East-West" system, along which natural resources travel from East to West, and high quality consumer or production commodities are transported from West to East. In other words, a transportation corridor should be created between Europe and Asia which, on the one hand, will become the shortest distance (or to be more precise, the cheapest) between these two continents, and on the other, all other conditions being equal, the safest. A significant portion of this corridor passes through the Southern Caucasus, in particular through the territory of two countries–Georgia and Azerbaijan (Gegeshidze, 1999A; Rondeli, 1999; Shevardnadze, 1999). It should be noted that when any transportation corridor is formed, accumulated experience should be taken into account, since our ancestors were guided by the same principles (short distances and transportation safety) as the people of our day and age. A graphic example is the historical Great Silk Road (Elisseeff, 2000; Foltz, 1999; Liu, 1998), on the principles of which the New Silk Road is to be built (Asadov, 2000; Gegeshidze, 1999B; Martirosian, 2000).

With respect to Georgia, in the "North-South" system, both the North (Russia) and the South (the Islamic world) are rich in various resources which compliment each other. Consequently, bilateral commodity flows in the "North-South" direction have certain prospects. But its implementation involves settling the acute Abkhazian problem. It is no secret that its resolution largely depends on Russia's stance, and to be more precise, on the political processes going on in this country.

In this way, of the two systems mentioned–"East-West" and "North-South"– only the first is currently economically (and not only economically) realistic for Georgia. This, all other conditions being equal, promotes prospects for the "East-South" and "West-South" systems, in which a third Southern Caucasian state, Armenia, is trying to find its niche. On the other hand, in light of the transportation corridor Europe-Caucasus-Asia project, Georgia is acquiring a very important international economic function, since it forms a significant portion of this corridor (Zvania, 1998). It is for this very reason that strategic investors are already paying it attention, since in this context the efficiency of investments made in Georgia is being defined not by the market dimensions of our republic or even of the entire Southern Caucasus. This transportation artery will make it possible to significantly expand these dimensions in two directions at the same time–to Europe and to Asia (Papava, 2002B, 2002D).

1.4. Georgia's Economic Lever

With respect to the Europe-Caucasus-Asia transportation corridor being developed, it is easy to explain why the decision was made to build one of the branches of the oil pipeline through Georgia for transporting early Caspian oil to the West. It is also understandable why the oil pipeline alternative Baku-Tbilisi-Ceyhan is also viewed as one of the most attractive when it comes to exporting major Caspian oil. This particular route possesses immense prospects, which will arouse the interest of strategic investors in our republic. The oil pipeline project is raising the feasibility of the above-mentioned "East-South" system, which is primarily expressed in the prospects for a gas pipeline between Azerbaijan and Turkey.

The transportation corridor Europe-Caucasus-Asia is currently shipping a large amount of freight by rail and via the seaports of Georgia. The volume of these shipments will increase. Recently, the question of building a major highway has become very pertinent.

Of course, the competence of the corridor is primarily related to developing transportation as a priority branch in the national economy, but it would be an enormous mistake to "reduce" the idea of the corridor to the fate of this branch alone. The task is much more complicated. The transportation corridor cannot function if a telecommunication system, power engineering, a network of hotels, and other service spheres are not created in the country. And this requires advancing branches necessary for the highly efficient development of the facilities listed above. The matter primarily concerns industry (which determines the industrial nature of the corridor itself) and agriculture (from the standpoint of providing foodstuffs).

Environmental protection and urbanization must be approached from a qualitatively different angle. On the one hand, the transportation corridor should not become a source of destructive influence on the environment, and on the other, efforts should be made to ensure that the country's entire population does not end up located along this corridor alone. In addition, as early as the planning stage, removing agricultural land from circulation should be kept to the minimum.

The influence of the transportation corridor on the national economy is not only restricted to the mentioned branches. It will have an impact on education (the training of personnel for the service sphere), public health (the construction of medical facilities along the corridor and in relevant large conurbation centers), and tourism (a widespread transportation and telecommunication network will create conditions for taking advantage of the rich natural landscape). What is more, additional possibilities will appear for scientific research which will stimulate applied work to ensure the corridor has the relevant technical level. The restored Great Silk Road will promote historical, ethnographical, economic, and other pursuits which are attractive from the viewpoint of becoming acquainted with the culture of the countries located along this route.

Consequently, the Europe-Caucasus-Asia transportation corridor will become an economic lever for Georgia and, in this way, will have more than just transportation significance, since it will encompass the entire national economy and the development strategy of each of its branches.

2

Impact of Inflation on Economic Growth: Lessons from Post-Communist Georgia

2.1. Political Request and Facts

The issue of inflation's impact on economic growth–both in general context and, specifically, in that of post-Communist transformation, has been a subject of numerous studies (see, for example, Allen, 1999; Anikin 2000; Anušić, Rohatin-ski, Šonje, and others (ed.), 1995; Asatiani, 2000; Cottarelli, Doele, 1999; Fisher, Sakhai, 1997; Cukrowski, 2000; Gaidar, 1997; Gamsakhurdia, 1997; Ghosh, Gulde, Ostry, Wolf, 1996; Jochem, 1999; Kakulia M., 2001A, 2001B; Kakulia, Aslamazishvili, 2000; Kakulia R., 1998; Kistauri, 2000; Klaus, 1997; Kornai, 1993; Kovzanadze, 2002, 2003; Krasavina (ed.), 2000; Managadze, 2002; Melo, Denizer, Gelb, 1997; Meskhia, 2000; Meskhia, Iashvili, 1998; Papava, 1997, 2000A; Patrytski, 2000; Schmieding, 1993; Sušjan, Lah, 1997; Wellisz, 1997; Zak (ed.), 1999; Zhirny, Yarochinskiy, 1997; Zukowski, 1996).

One of the most common themes that has often been subject to debate among the Georgian economist and political circles is the tight monetary policy pursued by the National Bank of Georgia (NBG), which is the key to both the stability of the exchange rate of national currency, the Lari, and a low inflation rate. Critics argue that such a monetary policy is a main obstacle that prevents the country from achieving greater economic growth and, therefore, insist that the government should increase money supply and, thereby, allow devaluation of Lari and a higher inflation rate. Such an attitude results from, on the one hand, unquestionable dilettantism in economics of those who propose such ideas and, on the other hand, an obvious interest of some of those critics in further expanding their already sizeable wealth–the source of which, by the way, is quite suspicious–through increased money supply, greater inflation rate and devaluated Lari.

Before we start discussing theoretical aspects of the problem (Papava, 1997, 2000A), let us touch on the alteration of key economic parameters in Georgia over the last couple of years and some of the reasons behind it.

Since the fall of 1994, owing to well-organized financial stabilization program, Georgia managed to escape from the hyperinflationary spiral (under which the inflation rate reached 50-70 percent a month). Furthermore, in 1995 the Georgian government implemented a successful currency reform and introduced a quite stable national currency, the Lari. In 1996-1997, after a long period of deep depression in 1989-1994, Georgian economy started growing and reached a quite high GDP growth rate. All this expressed in figures makes a very impressive picture: while in 1989-1994, as a result of decline, the status of economy deteriorated more than three times, in 1995 Gross Domestic Product (GDP) grew by 3.3 percent and in 1996 and 1997 by 11 percent and 10.8 percent respectively. During the same period, there were significant decreases in the rate of inflation: in 1995 it fell to 53 percent; in 1996 to 13.5; and in 1997 to as little as 7.3 percent (Papava, 1995, 1996, 1998, 1999; Papava, Beridze, 1998; Papava, Chikovani (ed.), 1997).

In 1998, the economic situation drastically deteriorated. This time, the slowdown was triggered by the renovation of hostilities in the Gali District of Abkhazia and a new tide of internally displaced persons fleeing their native region, the budgetary crisis resulted from government's mistakes in the finance policy, and the currency crisis sparked off by the turmoil in Russia's financial system. All these troubles were accompanied by a severe drought that dealt a serious blow to the country's agricultural and hydro energy sectors.

Even under such unfortunate circumstances, national economy kept moving upwards (even though this time the growth rate was really low–2.9 percent). Although the NBG started using its hard currency reserves to support commercial banks–which was the only correct step under the conditions of severe currency crisis–and replaced the regulated exchange rate of Lari with a floating currency regime, in 1998 the inflation rate never got out of hand and was stabilized at the level of 10.7 percent.

In 1999, due to the impetus inherited from economic developments of preceding years, the GDP growth rate was maintained at the level of 3.0 percent, whereas the annual inflation rate was fixed at 10.9 percent. It must be noted, however, that unless irresponsible forecasts about the expected fall of the Lari exchange rate and potential growth of inflation rate were made publicly by some high governmental officials in December 1998 and January 1999, which created in the country an atmosphere of upcoming inflation, the annual inflation rate could be even lower.

In 2000, economic growth made up 2.0 percent, whereas the inflation rate fell to 4.6 percent. In 2001, the same parameters changed to 4.5 and 3.4 percent respectively.

During the whole period, a serious change in the Lari exchange rate occurred just once–at the time of the currency crisis of 1998 (Kakulia, 2001B). Before and after that it remained more or less stable.

Thus, in 1998-1999, as a result of a 70-percent devaluation of Lari that took place in late 1998, the inflation rate exceeded a benchmark of 10 percent, whereas the GDP growth rate could not overcome a 3.0-percent limit, which means that there is no reason to believe that drastic devaluation of national currency and higher inflation rate have ever played any positive role in pushing the economy of post-Communist Georgia.

2.2. Where is the Mistake?

As was noted above, the most of critical remarks about the NBG were made in relation to its tight monetary policy the main goal of which was to keep inflation at a minimum level.

The opponents believe that the low inflation rate is an obstacle to the significant progress of production and the expansion of country's export potential and, in the long run, blocks the growth of exports. Accordingly, as they claim, time has come to say no to the tight monetary policy and replace it with a more liberal (or, at least, "moderately tight") approach, which will consist in a "controlled increase" in money supply.

Indeed, the economic theory admits that higher inflation rate may encourage production. Also, some historical examples have demonstrated that in some countries, under certain circumstances, the said approach was a success story in terms of production growth.

The two questions that must be asked, however, are these:

- Are Georgian companies really able to expand production under the conditions of high inflation rate?

- Will high inflation rate cause positive results for all spheres of economic life?

Only after getting satisfactory answers to the above questions one could consider the issue of switching to a "let go" policy.

Let us start with the question about whether or not our companies are able to develop under the conditions of high inflation rate. Unfortunately, we have to recognize from the very beginning that for a number of reasons the answer is a negative one.

The most of Georgian enterprises that come from the Communist epoch (like those in other republics of the former Soviet Union) own outdated equipment and technologies which can not produce competitive (high-quality and low-cost) goods. In other words, the share of "necroeconomy" (Papava, 2002E) in the overall national economy of Georgia is still very high. This means that unless serious investments are attracted and new (or renewed) markets are found (both of which needs time) it is senseless to even dream of the prosperity of those enterprises. Investments, in turn, could be attracted from the following three potential sources:

- company's own financial resources;

- bank loans;

- foreign investments.

The first source might be available for just a handful of enterprises (that have already found their foreign partners). The rest of the Georgian enterprises (which constitute a huge majority) suffer from serious financial hardships (enormous debts to the State budget and other enterprises).

As to bank loans, a few enterprises can afford them because of short term and high interest rates set by commercial banks for non-trade operations. Under the conditions of growing inflation, interest rates are likely to grow further leaving even less access to loans for companies involved in non-trade (and perhaps even trade) operations. Thus, neither the second source of investments can be used (especially in case of higher inflation rate) as a favorable condition for the production growth.

Foreign investments represent one of the most effective factors of improving Georgia's manufacturing potential. However, according to many experts, their flow into the Georgian economy has been a drawn-out process. The worldwide experience has shown that a time lag between the stabilization (of political and, especially, financial conditions) and the flow of considerable foreign investments into economy averages three years. Bearing in mind that since 1998 Georgia has permanently suffered from a deep budgetary crisis and the country's criminal record has drastically deteriorated over the last couple of years, one has to recognize that a potential foreign investment boom can only be anticipated three years after these problems will have been solved.

From the standpoint of foreign partners, growing inflation rate is very likely to be interpreted as a deviation from the stabilization course, in which case the flow of foreign investments into Georgian economy will be delayed for indefinite time. This means that under the conditions of higher inflation rate, nor the third source of production enhancing investments will be available.

Thus, in the Georgian context, an increased inflation rate not only is not likely to boost production, but also is likely to block access to those already scarce resources that still might be available for Georgian companies to enhance their non-trade operations.

Such a conclusion is more than enough to refute the assertion that a high inflation rate would boost production in Georgia. Nevertheless, complexity of the issue requires that special consideration be given to possible outcomes that the high inflation rate may produce in different sectors of economy.

First of all, let us touch on the issue of money circulation. Some ten years ago Georgia had no national currency at all. A huge majority of Georgian population and, what is particularly disappointing, the Georgian government people in charge at that time could not even imagine that Georgia could ever introduce and ensure proper regulation of its own currency. To illustrate this, it would suffice to recall the situation in early 1993, when Russia, by quitting supply of ruble bills to Georgia (that by then had already proclaimed independence), caught unawares the Government of Georgia; furthermore, in April 1993, some representatives of the same government publicly apologized to the people for having to introduce a transitional national currency, the Georgian Coupon; in fact, it was a public confession of their inability to endow the Coupon with the functions of money. If you add to this unrestrained lending (for various "generous" reasons) that pushed Georgia into the spiral of hyperinflation, it will be no surprise that at that time nobody believed that we would ever be able to have our own currency and a normal lending system. In the meantime, increasingly louder were getting voices of those people (especially at the higher government echelons) who insisted that Georgia should have begged Russia to be merciful and admit us into the "ruble zone".

Although a tight monetary policy initiated in the fall of 1994 enabled us to curb inflation, implement a successful currency reform and maintain a stable exchange rate for the newly introduced national currency, the Lari, gloomy memories of the recent past have stuck in people's minds and prevent them from accepting it as a reliable currency. Specifically, people's confidence in Lari, as a means of accumulation, is still very fragile; that's why particularly costly objects (such as houses, flats, vehicles, land parcels) which could not be purchased without accumulated funds are usually sold for US Dollars.

Under such circumstances, the growing inflation rate will finally undermine the people's already little trust in Lari as a means of accumulation. Furthermore, it will diminish the effect that has already been achieved: while today the Lari is used everywhere in the retailing network, tomorrow with the growing inflation rate the situation may change to the opposite.

As long as prices are kept at a relatively low level, in exchange there should be involved not only low-value Lari bills, but also coins. To the extent that in Georgia low-value Dollar bills, like those of other hard currencies, are in short supply, whereas US coins are not available at all, and that after the devaluation of Russian Rouble confidence in it fell noticeably, both the Lari and the Tetri (the Georgian coins) have no real "competitor" in sales and purchases of low-and medium-value goods and services. If the inflation rate goes up such an advantage of the Lari (and especially the Tetri) will be lost (note that one-and two-Tetri coins have already been removed from circulation) and the Lari's standing as opposed to that of the ruble will weaken. The reason is that Russia's negative influence on the situation in Georgia is still very strong: at the Russian military bases salaries are paid in Roubles (through the Russian military Bank). Companies located at those bases also receive donations from the same source in Roubles. To the Georgian Government's repeated protests against such practices the Russian party paid no attention. It is impossible to predict when such a monetary sabotage could be eliminated and civilized forms of banking relationships with Russia could be established.

Thus, at this moment unleashed inflation will lead to the diminution of the Lari coverage area and encourage the use of the US Dollar and the Russian Rouble for accumulating and retailing purposes respectively.

Under the conditions of a higher inflation rate, it will be more difficult to reform the real sector, namely to implement restructuring and privatization programs in this sector, as the growing inflation rate puts the brakes on such developments.

Under the conditions of a higher inflation rate, the country's general social picture will become gloomier.

Finally, under the conditions of a higher inflation rate, the people's living conditions, all other things being equal, will inevitably deteriorate. This process may be less painful in those countries where minimum wage is at least 1.5 times or twice higher than subsistence minimum. In this country, however, where minimum wage makes just a low percentage of subsistence minimum (not to mention wages and pensions being many months in arrears), the growing inflation rate will strike badly at the most vulnerable groups in out society which make up not less than a quarter of the whole population in Georgia. Even based on the most optimistic forecasts, minimum wage, not to mention minimum pension, will not exceed subsistence minimum for the foreseeable future, which can not be taken as an argument for a "let go" policy in favor of inflation.

Consequently, there is no reason to believe that even relatively easy monetary policy could produce any positive results for Georgia.

In conclusion, let us touch on the issue why it is so important to keep a stable exchange rate for the Lari. While the devaluation of Lari is likely to increase customs revenues, it will inevitably lead to the growth of foreign debt servicing costs as well. For a small country like Georgia, where imports play a leading role in external trade, the devaluation of Lari will cause the enlargement of import costs and, thereby stimulate inflation, potential negative results of which were discussed above.

All positive and negative effects of the devaluation of Lari need to be offset against each other. The country's present economic situation (and, first of all, deep fiscal crisis which unfortunately has not been overcome so far) makes it obvious that negative effects still prevail over positive ones.

3

Russian Scenario of the Global Economic Crisis and Georgia's Strategy

3.1. Russian Scenario of the US Dollar Crisis

The horrible act of terrorism of 11th September 2001 against the USA has been a tremendous shock to the whole world. However, this event and the ensuing consequences are likely to have an even greater impact on the international economy.

Debates concerning the stability of the US Dollar and the chances for America to maintain, together with its economy, a leading position in the world in the long run, had started long before the drama of 11th September.

Let us consider a scenario providing a quite sensational prognosis suggested by Russian experts insisting on the inevitability of the downfall of the US Dollar (Khazin, Grigoriev, 2001). What is this prognosis based on?

Growing imbalances between the "new" (informational) and "old" (traditional industrial) sectors are regarded as factors provoking a global crisis. While income generation in the "old economy" has remained at a comparatively moderate and at the same time stable growth rate, in the "new economy" it has been rising at rates of up to 10 per cent per month (Khazin, Grigoriev, 2001, p. 16).

It is noteworthy that in the economic report of President Clinton before the US Congress made on 12th January 2001 the most attention in the national economy was drawn to the leading role of the "new economy", however, this phenomenon (as well as its definition) has not yet been fully explored (see, for example, Deikin, 2001, p. 3). This is not surprising, given that many American theorists have expressed doubts about introduction of the term "new economy" (Deikin, 2001, p. 22). In particular, it is still being analyzed on a theoretical level whether the "new economy" is an advanced phase of the postindustrial society or a new one–an "upper postindustrial" stage (Deikin, 2001, p. 20).

Despite this, let us try to specify the meaning of the "new economy" (see, for example, ECE, 2000, pp. 3-5).

One of the significant features of the "new economy" (e.g. Internet technology) is that it requires huge primary investment, the benefits from which may be realized only through a very large scale development of a given project. Starting from the initial level of profitability, even a slight increase in investment is then likely to stimulate a significant growth in profits. At the same time, some controversy has arisen concerning profitability and productivity; in particular, from the very beginning there was high expectation that the "new economy" might facilitate a sharp rise in the level of productivity but this did not occur: it was the Nobel Prize laureate Prof. Robert Solow, who was the first to express doubts concerning the important role of computerization in the growth of productivity, which were recently proved by empirical estimations performed by other American economists (Deikin, 2001, pp. 22-23).

According to the assessment by Bill Gates–a living legend of the computer business–if the previous epochs of economic development were characterized by evolutionists as a long-term stability with short-term revolutionary interventions, called "an interrupted equilibrium", today electronic information is creating a permanently changeable environment, which he refers to as "interrupted chaos" (Gates, 1999, ch. VI).

It is interesting that, while the prices for "old economy" products are determined by demand and supply, the prices for "new economy" products are dependent on the future yield.

As a result, in contrast to the old economy, the new economy follows a divergent, so-called "investment" pattern. This is when large initial costs are borne by those investors who expect the highest returns over a relatively long period. Moreover, on the stock exchange the equity value of the "new economy" companies is defined from future, in a sense, "virtual" profit and not from the current balance of income and expenditure (Khazin, Grigoriev, 2001, p. 19).

As stated by the authors of the proposed scenario, this hampers stock market stability, as it displays the features of a financial pyramid and its sustainability is based on psychology.

Insofar as the initial base of the "new economy" assets is rather dubious, any essential slowdown in the stock market growth rates is likely to entail a large-scale crisis.

The study underlines that after the upturn of the 70's of the 20th Century the continuing stable economic growth of the US derived from the collapse of the USSR and the US expansion into its former markets on the one hand, and the creation of the "new economy", which "pulled over" extensive financial resources on the other hand. Hence, the USA returned the phenomenon of the 20's of the 20th Century—fast economic growth without inflation.

The authors acknowledge the peculiarity of the American case, when the "old economy" had started to lose in competition against the "new economy" for credits and investment and in the labor market, leading to an increase in the cost of factors of production which in its turn affected overall production costs (Khazin, Grigoriev, 2001, p. 23).

Thus, a steady decline in the relative profitability of the "old economy" with the ensuing outcomes is regarded as a "release mechanism" for the global economic crisis. In particular, should producers raise prices they will fail to compete with importers, resulting in growth of imports and deterioration of the trade balance deficit; while in case of maintaining supply at low prices local producers will face a real danger of loss.

Following this scenario, a substantial enlargement of financial capacity of the "new economy" resulted in a reduction in the share of savings and an upsurge in consumption provoking inflationary processes along with the rise of interest rates. An additional factor, which intensified the inflationary process is the appreciation of the USD against other currencies resulting in import stimulation. In particular, during the 7-months period of 2001 the trade balance deficit reached US 20.6 billion Dollars which is 46 per cent in excess of the same indicator for the relevant period of the past year (Khazin, Grigoriev, 2001, p. 24).

Inasmuch as imports begin to dominate over consumption and US companies refuse to contract production in order to avoid a risk of their shares falling, start to stockpile (with stock substantially growing–by some 1 per cent of the GDP per quarter) and publicly present this as expansion of production, there is a danger of "excessive" production (Khazin, Grigoriev, 2001, p. 25).

An important factor which is expected to intensify the above-described processes is the colossal amount of US Dollars and securities placed outside the USA available for return at the first sign of a global crisis.

Under the given scenario, proceeding from the analysis of the stock market the "Dow Jones" (of a traditional sector) and "NASDAQ" (of a high technology sector) indexes should no longer have an objective basis for growth, which is an indication that profitability of investment in the US stock market has diminished. At the same time, the variation of indices has become wider pointing towards the speculative behavior of "market makers".

It is interesting to mention that the US stock market is given a similar appraisal by other Russian experts (Doronin, Zagashvili, Pripisnov, 2001). According to them, the fall in the price of shares of high technology "growth companies" at the end of 2000 and the beginning of 2001 was caused by (Doronin, Zagashvili, Pripisnov, 2001):

- excessive capitalization; the share of high technology companies in total sales and employment did not exceed 10 per cent of the corresponding indicator for non-financial companies, it represented 36 percent of US stock market capitalization;

- ineffective use of the attracted capital; namely, in 1995-1999 80 per cent out of US 150 billion Dollars was spent by the US Internet companies on advertising, investment banks' fees for primary distribution of shares and on subsidizing the cost of the services offered;

- the speculative nature of the up-trend on the high technology stock market causing over valuation of the "growth companies".

It is noteworthy that, according to an assessment by the Merill Lynch experts, the fall in share prices in the USA is likely to be followed by a fall in consumption by up to US 100 billion Dollars, in its turn resulting in 1 per cent reduction of the GDP (Doronin, Zagashvili, Pripisnov, 2001). It is interesting that half of the total shares in the USA is owned by individuals. Owing to this, devaluation of "paper assets" may significantly change current consumption which will tell on demand and exacerbate (and perhaps prolong) a potential economic crisis (Rubtsov, 2001, p. 44).

According to this Russian scenario of the US Dollar crisis, November 2001 was identified as the beginning of the economic crisis, as this is the time when traditionally, enterprises publish their quarterly statements of balance (Khazin, Grigoriev, 2001, p. 29). Under the scenario, if by this time the rate of inflation is high, the US Dollar shall experience further depreciation.

According to one of the authors of this scenario–Michael Khazin, EURO 0.96-0.97/USD 1 is a critical rate; upon reaching this level the exchange of global holdings of US Dollars into EURO could be much accelerated resulting in the fall of share prices which in its turn shall provoke a large-scale international economic crisis (Kvitko, 2001, p. 7).

The conclusions presented in this scenario with regard to the effects of the crisis are quite pessimistic (Khazin, Grigoriev, 2001, pp. 29-32):

First, collapse of the exchange market by various estimates could entail a loss of US 7-15 trillion Dollars. At the same time, it would lose its function of the "hot money" neutralizer further intensifying inflationary processes and leading to the return to the USA of the Dollars accumulated outside the country after World War II.

Second, financial institutions, the biggest part of whose assets consist of securities, would be bankrupt.

Third, budgetary incomes diminish which in its turn would be reflected in the reduction of financing for social programs. With a 1.5-3 times reduction in average consumption throughout the world, a cutback of private consumption in order to recover a long-term saving rate would still lower living standards in the USA.

Fourth, collapse of the World Trade Organization (WTO) would be inevitable and this will encourage protectionism. Under such circumstances, the US Dollar shall lose its function of an international currency while the EURO is not yet in the position to replace it. As a result, a multicurrency system in the world would be restored.

Fifth, countries would shift to the budgetary crediting of production. While raising competitiveness of native production this shall also serve as an impulse to the growth of inflation.

Sixth, the major exporters to America such as Japan, China and countries of South-East Asia and Russia and the countries of Latin America shall suffer a damage, the former–through reduction of exports to the USA and the latter–through depreciation of the US Dollar (as for them it is a parallel currency).

As we know, in the short-term there is a positive correlation between the markets of the USA and most of the developed and developing countries (Rubtsov, 2001, p. 41), providing a base for a large-scale distribution of this crisis. If one generation ago it took weeks and even months for the stock and currency crisis to expand, now when the world financial market is based on electronic contacts, the speed of the crisis distribution has been reduced to one day (Gates, 1999, ch. VI).

The authors of this scenario consider that, provided Russia creates a relatively flexible Labor Code and succeeds in assuring investors of the immutability of "the rules of the game" then, given a highly qualified work force, it would be possible to invest free capital released from the US financial markets in Russian natural resources (Khazin, Grigoriev, 2001, pp. 29-31).

However, in our opinion it is rather doubtful that there will be any large-scale investment given the high level of corruption, existence of a high risk factor and low protection of foreign investors.

3.2. Russian Vision on the Economic Policy Exercised in China

Since under the considered Russian scenario of the US Dollar crisis, protectionism is expected to prosper, the Russian experts regard the practice of financial and economic policy exercised in China as rather attractive in providing maximum protection from the anticipated global crisis. However, it is notable that there is a progressive trend in the present day China which is openly aimed at reaching economic and perhaps even political domination over the rest of the world and the key slogan is "XXI century–is the century of China" (Gelbras, Kuznetsov, 2001, p. 119).

The Chinese financial strategy, positively appraised by the Russian experts, can be characterized as follows (Anisimov, 2001, pp. 124-138):

- a comparatively high level of regulation of price-formation (sectors producing raw-material are fully state-owned allowing the state to control prices by stimulating exporters on one hand and through protection of home produce by customs-tariffs on the other);

- average level of Tax Burden and customs-tariffs encouraging economic competition;

- high concentration of physical persons providing large financial inflow in credit institutions;

- performance of a function of a large investor by the state (total amount of state credits totals on average USD 3 billion p.a. of which medium and long-term credits issued exceed USD 1 billion);

- managed exchange system which also implies two currencies: firstly, Hong Kong Dollar efficiently used on foreign markets and a relatively "soft" but on the whole sufficiently "strong" Yuan.

It should be mentioned that the state executive system and financial and economic structure of China is so specific that it is less possible to "replicate" this pattern to other states. However, it should also be taken into account that as the history proves undertaking a number of significant functions of a market on behalf of the Government puts under question sustainability of this pattern in the long-run.

In order to make an assessment of the Russian scenario of the US Dollar crisis discussed above it should be underlined that the processes described therein have been long known, which is no wonder at least because the specialists are well aware of a gradual fall of the NASDAQ index and also the reasons provoking such fall. We consider that the weakest point of the scenario prepared by Russian specialists is over-dramatization of the events, by assuming that the current strains in the economy of the USA will inevitably grow into Dollar crisis and global economic collapse.

Although we partially agree with the main approaches presented in this scenario, but it is difficult to share the idea that the Dollar crisis has definitely been caused by development of new technologies. In particular, the main arguments in favor of the "new economy" are that new information technologies and market liberalization have changed the principal macroeconomic interrelation between expansion of production, inflation and unemployment. New technologies ensure more effective management of reserves; enhanced management of information flows allows a more economical use of resources while the Internet provides the consumer with a wider choice of products and increasing competitiveness, which then things being equal finally leads to low inflation (ECE, 2000, pp. 2-5).

3.3. Modification of the Russian Scenario in the Conditions of Antiterrorist War

The Russian scenario of the US Dollar crisis does not allow for correction of the above-mentioned processes by possible wars (Khazin, Grigoriev, 2001, p. 33).

With a qualitatively new antiterrorist war having broken out in the world today, there are naturally questions arising with regard to the possibility of global economic crisis and whether the USA will retain its economic hegemony in the world.

The answer to these questions depends on the scale of this antiterrorist campaign and its territorial spread. Two scenarios could be considered:

First, limiting the antiterrorist campaign to Afghanistan and Iraq, and if (as in fact was the case) on behalf of the terrorists there are no response assaults on the USA or allied states. Otherwise, this antiterrorist war initiated by the USA would have acquired the features of the war waged by the USA against Vietnam or Iraq (in early 90s of 20th century) or that of the NATO against Yugoslavia.

The economy of the USA may perhaps even benefit from such a course of events as regards the unfavorable symptoms of excessive production, since in the conditions of war military needs may "drain" it of excessive financial and material resources, hence the further extension of the stage of economic upturn. In addition, the claiming of the leadership of the antiterrorist campaign by the USA and its continuation had to some extent prepared companies and the population to take account of the risk of war in their decisions. Thus, according to the first scenario a global economic crisis is practically excluded.

As for the *second* scenario let us consider the case whereby there might occur successive acts of international terrorism and that the fight against it goes beyond the boundaries of one particular state.

Taking into account that, in case of expansion of terrorist aggression, it would be quite difficult to defeat international terrorism by means of so-called "targeted attacks", events may develop in a quite complicated way.

Firstly, if against the background of antiterrorism operations the terrorists again succeed in committing any impressive act of aggression this may seriously undermine confidence in the effectiveness of these operations as well as their main performer–the United States. If this happens it will most probably result in the loss of trust in financial institutions of the USA. In particular, the notion of the omnipotence of the United States and its currency may be damaged, resulting in a notable contraction of the extent of use of the US Dollar as an internationally applicable means of settlement.

Anyway, the immediate signs of this trend unfortunately, could have been observed during the last decade: if for 1989 the share of the USD in the total exchange markets turnover was 45 per cent, for 1995 it has made up just 41.5 per cent (while the share of the USA in the GDP world-wide is 20.7 per cent and in world exports–15.2 per cent); similar indicators for European Union are correspondingly, 20.4 and 14.7 per cent; during the relevant period, the share of DM increased from 13.5 to 18.5 per cent and that of the French Franc form 1 to 4 per cent; impact of Swiss Franc decreased from 5 to 3.5 per cent; as to Japanese Yen, it fluctuated within 13.5-12 per cent (Tavlas, 2001, p. 4). It is interesting that for 1996-2000 the analysis of the growth rates of M2 gives the same picture: in particular, in 1996-2000 in the USA M2 fell by 4.7 per cent, while on the contrary M2 increased by 47.9 per cent for Japan, by 47 for the EURO zone, by 47 per cent for Great Britain, by 39.7 per cent for the Asian Four (Korea, Singapore, Taiwan and Hong Kong) and by 3 per cent for Switzerland (IMF, 2001A, p. 802; IMF, 2001B, p. 216). It should also be taken into account that appreciation of the major world currencies was not of inflationary nature and was mainly predetermined by the extension of the international area of their application; for instance, in Japan, in 1996-2000 there was a 6.6 per cent deflation against an essential growth of monetary aggregates (by 47.9 per cent). As concerns Great Britain, during the relevant period a rise in prices had insignificantly exceeded that of the USA and made up 13.6 per cent, the growth of monetary aggregates was much more significant, though (47 per cent) (IMF, 2001B, p. 205). Following these trends, a further constriction of the area of application of the USD is to be expected.

Secondly, a negative balance of payments of the USA may continue to grow in the short-term which, together with the reduction of the area of application of the US Dollar, may provoke its devaluation.

Thirdly, the antiterrorist campaign of the USA shall to some extent result in utilization of the excess resources and postpone a possible crisis of excessive production.

Fourthly, the demand of the US Government for the production of safety measures on high technologies shall increase causing a "diversion" of private investments to state investments (the effect of "crowding out" of private investments by state ones). In its turn, this may stimulate a rise of interest rates which, considering the high transparency of the economy of USA would cause a perceptible growth of capital inflow, leading to the improvement of the balance of capital movement and correspondingly, to appreciation of the USD again (though, it may be difficult to return its position of primacy).

Fifth, aviation and insurance have suffered serious damage which may also have effects on other sectors as well. It might be that insurance and re-insurance companies generally increase the rates of insurance premium, ultimately resulting in an increase of production costs and hence, in price rises.

One of the most serious forms of aggression is via computer through which terrorists try to disrupt electronic connections in various fields. In case of use of this form of aggression in financial markets, a world-wide financial and economic crisis would be inevitable.

Under the second discussed scenario, with the antiterrorist war underway a possibility of evading a global economic crisis is largely dependent on the success of military actions by the USA and its partner countries and on the perfection and timeliness of the preventive antiterrorism measures on their part. The success of the antiterrorist operations carried out in Afghanistan and Iraq has much lowered the potential for a second occurrence.

3.4. Georgia's Strategy

Regarding the trend of developments in the world, a significant rise in prices for oil is not very likely to occur. As regards a moderate rise, this could be reflection of the increase of insurance components in costs of oil production and transportation on one hand and of certain delays in supply on the other hand. It should also be underlined that the possibility of carrying out acts of terrorism by terrorists against oil-producing Islamic countries is practically excluded as this would deprive them of a potential justification to declare "Jehad"–a religious war–against the West.

Proceeding from the above-referred, it is dubious whether this will contribute an additional argument on economic advantages to the political attractiveness of the investment Baku-Tbilisi-Ceyhan project of the oil pipeline.

Taking into account that Georgia is a small economy it is not in a position to influence global economic developments, but pursuing a more or less reasonable economic policy may even bring certain benefits, though, if we say nothing about minimization of the impact of negative effects.

It is unlikely that antiterrorist hostilities would somehow hamper functioning of the Georgian transport corridor for a definite period. If this is to happen anyway, it will provide a certain argument for the development of Russian transport links and Russia will naturally make the maximum use of this opportunity.

The fact that under the decision of the US Government, the American military already undertook preparation of Georgian army units for carrying out antiterrorist operations will qualitatively improve the national security situation which in its turn, will contribute to the further increase of the international role of the Georgian transport corridor.

It is worth noting that, in the war of the USA against terrorism, the understanding and support of such Europe-oriented Islamic countries as Turkey and Azerbaijan has been growing. This would further increase the international role of the Georgian transport corridor for transportation of energy resources from Azerbaijan to Turkey.

Naturally, when Russian experts regard the perspective of a global economic crisis as inevitable (which in our opinion is somewhat exaggerated), questions arise concerning Georgia's monetary policy in case of a possible devaluation of the USD and the advantages and disadvantages of maintaining the current rate of the Georgian currency–Lari.

One of the important characteristics of the post-Communist economy is a large-scale shadow economy mostly "served" by the USD. The shadow economy would suffer most in case of a significant devaluation of the USD, which does not presently entail its substitution by legal economy as this last is, though relatively less, but still is quite dependent on the US Dollar. In Georgia the share of statistically unrecorded production in total output was 35 per cent in 2002, while in the entrepreneurial sector the indicators are correspondingly, 56.0 per. cent (SDSG, 2002, p. 5). A severe devaluation of the USD would place almost one third of Georgian economy (i.e. shadow economy) and over half of the entrepreneurial sector under the risk of total destruction. As regards shifting to the legal sector, it will be prevented by a similar situation inside the shadow economy, when as of 2002, deposit liabilities and the amount of loans in the USD issued to non-governmental sector from the banking system exceeds 80 per cent (SDSG, 2002, pp. 29, 31).

For the legal sector of the Georgian economy a positive effect resulting from the possible devaluation of the USD is the reduction of the Lari equivalent of the amount of the foreign debt representing a relief for the State Budget of Georgia.

At the same time there are negative effects that should also be regarded.

Firstly, import stimulation which would further increase the deficit in the balance of payments;

Secondly, reduction of tax incomes to the Budget from foreign investments;

Thirdly, less possibilities of covering budgetary liabilities from external sources.

Georgia faced certain challenges, owing to the financial crisis in Turkey, its major trading partner. However, thanks to the support by the IMF the tension has relieved.

We believe that, along with tightening customs control, Georgia should introduce certain restrictions based on international quality standards so as both to protect the interests of consumers in Georgia and to achieve an improvement of the balance of payments.

It is important to maintain stability of the exchange rate of the Lari.

In a situation of a possible devaluation of the US Dollar, diversification of the currency reserves by the NBG is regarded very important, presently counting all more or less stable currencies in these reserves.

According to the idea of some experts, in view of the confrontation between United States and their allies and the Islamic terrorists, it is likely that the highest stability will be preserved by those currencies of those countries which are less involved in military action. First of all this includes Japanese yen and Swiss Franc. Hence, currency reserves of the NBG should reflect a five-pole economy (USD, EURO, Yen, Pound Sterling, Swiss Franc).

Taking into account the fact that the value of the IMF unit of account–Special Drawing Rights (SDR), in contrast to the component currencies, is characterized by high stability, the second model of the currency reserves of the NBG can be based on the SDR structure; In particular, to achieve maximum security of these reserves the "basket" should have the same composition as the SDR with regard to the percentage of each comprising currency (see, for example, IMF, 2003).

It is important to note that the NBG recommended to commercial banks and generally to all private entities to diversify their deposits in order to minimize risk (Papava, Chocheli, 2002).

4

Prospects for the Formation of the "Three-Pole World Exchange System" and Georgia

4.1. George Soros Against the US Dollar

In an environment of world-wide globalization, practically any individual country will to an increasing extent feel the impact of the ongoing economic processes in the international economy. This is the case even more so, with the world financial system based on electronic communications and on-line distribution and sharing of information as a factor of production.

In this chapter, we discuss an opinion of the famous multi-millionaire and philanthropist, George Soros, stating that in the near future the US Dollar is likely to lose one third of its value (see, for example, Ananova, 2002). In his opinion, confidence in the US Administration's economic management has been undermined throughout the world.

Merrill Lynch experts, who think that the rate of Euro by the end of 2003 will have reached 1.25, make almost a similar prognosis and their colleagues from "Gold Sachs" go even further predicting EUR/USD 1.35 (see, for example, Mikhailovich, 2003, p. 13).

According to George Soros, depreciation of the US Dollar will affect the world economy and the scandals in regard to accounting and corporate frauds in certain major American companies will stimulate an outflow of capital from the USA.

This statement has given rise to a new wave of debates concerning future prospects of the US Dollar and the US economy, as a whole. About ten years ago Soros made a similar statement with regard to the British Pound Sterling as well. He conversed his assets in Pound Sterling to start purchasing when its rate had reached minimum value, thus gaining high profits (see, for example, Pravda, 1999).

Although we could perhaps partly share these forecasts, it seems less probable that events will develop in such a dramatic way and that the US Dollar will experience such a strong devaluation, otherwise it would create a threat to the international exchange system and hence, to normal functioning of the world economy.

It should be noted that the USA, Japan and the Euro zone produce 45.3 per cent of the world GDP and they also account for 42.8 per cent of the world imports and 40.9 per cent of exports (Iša, 2002, p. 13). Severe economic shocks in these countries might provoke an economic crisis all over the world and this is neither in the interests of the countries in question nor any other countries.

A successful peace operation in Iraq would have a positive impact on the ongoing economic processes both in the USA and the rest of the world. In particular, it would influence real earnings of the population and gains of corporations who will benefit from a steady fall in prices for energy resources. However, should partisan warfare persist on whatever scale, Iraq is likely to lose any attractiveness for investment.

4.2. Why a "Three-Pole World Exchange System"?

There is no doubt that a wave of corporate crises that first occurred in Great Britain in 1995-1999, and which at the end of 2002 overtook the United States, has to a great extent destroyed the myth of the omnipotence of the American economy and weakened the position of the US Dollar on the international scene. Nevertheless, a look into history will convince us that it is too early for the US Dollar to be "written off". However, at the first sight, a pure American problem has initiated formation of a "three-pole world exchange system" in the world which, we believe, will become of paramount importance for establishing the subsequent exchange order in the world. What are grounds for drawing such conclusions?

Prognosis that introduction of the common European currency–Euro would somewhat shaken the leading positions of the US Dollar have come true. As concerns the initial depreciation of the Euro, it was only temporary and the following economic developments have proved the validity of the above-referred assumptions.

In May 23 2003, the Euro was 1.1837 against the US Dollar, by 1 cent exceeding the value of 1.1747 in January 1, 1999 to which the history of the Euro dates back. However, it should be noted that the above-referred value is still slightly below the maximum quotation of the rate of Euro (1.1906) (Mikhailovich, 2003).

It is also worth noting, that a hypothetical rate of the Euro during the past decade, being calculated on the basis of the currencies comprising the Euro basket, is somewhat higher than the maximum quotation of the Euro.

As estimated by the vice-president of the European Central Bank Lucas Papademos, the maximum rate of the Euro is close to the average hypothetical rate of the Euro for the past 15 years (USA Today, 2003). This allows us to suppose that the Euro still has a potential for further appreciation. It should also be taken into account that transfer to the common European currency has entailed a significant reduction in transaction costs between the currencies of these countries while conversion costs are now zero, thereby to some extent increasing its potential for further appreciation. Moreover, free movement of goods and services, capital and labor will contribute to the more effective distribution of resources.

However, it is unclear on one hand whether a further devaluation of the US Dollar is reasonable and on the other hand, how acceptable a "cheap" Dollar is for the economy of the European Community, Japan and other developed countries.

The answer will be definitely negative, as a significant devaluation of the US Dollar would set off a cascade of devaluation processes in its major trade partners, finally leading us to the increase of protectionism and downturn of economic activity in the world (Papava, Chocheli, 2002).

Proceeding from the above-said, an effective appreciation of the Euro is less acceptable and the parity against the US Dollar fixed at the time of introduction of the Euro will either be maintained or may slightly increase.

Although the economic situation in Europe is much better, a further strengthening of the Euro would diminish competitiveness of European goods both on home and foreign markets. Obviously, an "expensive" Euro will lead to weakening of exports, though this will be compensated with cheap imports.

Further rise of the Euro will endanger economic growth in the Euro zone. In the first quarter of 2003, there was no overall economic growth recorded in the Euro zone and an economic recession in Germany, whose economy is the largest in Europe, was reflected in a growth rate of 0.2 per cent (USA Today, 2003).

In contrast to the Euro zone, in the United States the growth of GDP was 1.9 per cent, exceeding the preliminary projections by 0.3 per cent. According to "The Economist" estimates, during 2003-2004, economic growth in the United States will be at 5.6 per cent level and in Japan and Germany it is projected at 1.5 and 3.1 per cent, respectively (see, for example, Episheva, 2003, p. 26).

Unlike the Federal Reserve System of the USA, the European Central Bank has a cushion (reduction of the interest rate) for maintaining stability of its currency and ensuring parity of terms of trade. The session of the European Central Bank of 5 July 2003 decided upon a 0.5 per cent reduction of the rate to 2 per cent, which will stimulate economic activity in Europe on one hand and cause a capital outflow from the Euro zone and somewhat neutralize appreciation of the European currency.

Further enlargement of the Euro zone through involving Great Britain, would serve as an additional short-term influence for the stability of the Euro, as Great Britain is experiencing approximately twice the rate of economic growth of the Euro zone countries and the target is to attain 2.2 per cent growth in 2003 (Britain USA, 2003). However, as recently underlined by the Chancellor of the Exchequer (Minister of Finance), Gordon Brown, five tests intended for Great Britain, which were supposed to ascertain its readiness to enter the Euro zone, have produced negative results, postponing its accession for an indefinite period of time (Economist, 2003).

It is reasonable to discuss those factors that will have various impacts on the economy of the USA and will in perspective influence probable dynamics of the US Dollar. Let us first consider circumstances accounting for the depreciation of the US Dollar.

The *first* is shrinking of confidence in the US economy, which will contribute to the weakening of the US Dollar position in the commodities markets and lessening of the share of the US Dollar in central bank reserves. Until recently, trading of oil and gold was carried out in US Dollars and approximately 50 per cent of the central bank reserves were held in US Dollars (BBC, 2002).

The effects of some of the circumstances which have encouraged us to draw such conclusions, still exist. This is the growing collision between the "old" and "new" economies. That is, the price of the shares of the "new economy" companies on stock exchanges is determined not on the basis of statement of current incomes and expenses but by future "virtual" profits. (Khazin, Grigoriev, 2001, p. 19). This situation is impeding stability of stock exchanges, as far as it is exhibiting some features of a financial pyramid and its stability is underpinned by psychology. Bankruptcy of such giant corporations as Enron Corp., WorldCom Inc. and a catastrophic fall in the cost of the shares of others was a tremendous shock to the whole world. However, in addition to the initial accounting nature of the crisis, it has equally involved auditing service, stock market regulators, commercial banks, rating agencies and corporate management. It is also noteworthy that, owing to a high degree of openness of the USA economy it will have a great effect on the economic situation in other leading countries, as well.

Here we had a case of the so-called "Bubble Economy" explained as a situation when there is an agitated demand, and prices for securities and real estate are boosted (see, for example, Bok Zi Kou, 2002, p. 178; Nariai, 2002, pp. 56-57).

It is to be noted that the above-referred characteristics of the economy do not encompass a separate segment but rather have a macroeconomic effect and predetermine a significant impact on a monetary and fiscal system of the country.

Second, corporate scandals have significantly distorted balance of capital of the USA, which found its reflection both in increasing capital outflow and decreasing capital inflow.

During the recent period, the balance of payments of the USA has had a large deficit (5 per cent of the GDP). Until recently, the deficit was covered through net capital inflow. While in 1999, 91 per cent of the current account deficit was financed through foreign direct investments, by 2002 this indicator has fallen to 43 per cent (Economist, 2002, p. 69). The experts consider that this downtrend will persist. The above-referred downtrend has been pre-conditioned by a lack of confidence in the US economy on one part and by selling foreign assets on behalf of American investors (e.g. ordinary Euro zone shares), on the other.

Third, depreciation of the US Dollar persuades foreign investors to sell securities and shares which results in a decrease in their price. It is well known that foreigners possess 40 per cent of the T-Bills of the USA as well as one third of other securities and 13 per cent of real estate (Economist, 2002, p. 70).

As concerns factors preventing devaluation of the USA Dollar, they are:

First, shrinking of the share of the US Dollar in international reserves would have been more sensible save for the behavior of the major trade partners of America directed at preventing depreciation of the USA Dollar and hence, deterioration of the conditions of trade in foreign economic relations; no doubt that "expensive" Euro or Yen will cause a reduction in exports. Therefore, they are increasing the share of the US Dollar in their currency reserves. In particular, the Central Bank of Japan has purchased USD 43 billion (the largest currency operation in recent years), South Korea and Taiwan–USD 4.5 billion; in March 2003, the same indicator for China was USD 7.8 billion (Gazeta, 2003).

However, recently in currency interventions targeted at attaining stability of currency rates, the priority has been given to collective interventions. The analysis made by the Professor of the University of Tokyo Takatoshi Ito, showed that joint interventions by central banks of various countries in the 1990s proved 20-50 times more effective than intervention made by the Central Bank of Japan alone (Economist, 2002, p. 69).

Second, an insignificant depreciation of the US Dollar will stimulate exports of the United States, increase corporate profits and investment; at the same time facilitating implementation of structural reforms and corporate restructuring in the Euro zone and Japan, thus raising efficiency in the regions and benefiting the international economy as well. In particular, according to one of the estimates, 20 per cent depreciation of the US Dollar will cause a 1 per cent growth throughout the world (Economist, 2002, p. 70). However, as noted above, such depreciation is less expected.

Although until lately, there was a one-pole international exchange system, recent developments have established a basis for a "three-pole world exchange system" (USA Dollar, Euro and Yen). However, gold as an international reserve asset has become of paramount importance again. As underlined by Professor Hans Tietmeyer, former President of the Deutsche Bundesbank, gold accounts for about EUR 40 billion (15 per cent) of reserves of the Central Bank of Europe and 10.5 per cent of international reserves of Russia (Gold, 2001). This trend persists in other countries as well.

In addition, the positions of the countries of Latin America and Asia insist on increasing the role of the Euro in the framework of international exchange reform. For instance, in the MERCOSUR countries of Latin America and countries of ASEAN+3 (China, Japan and Korea), they attentively follow regional monetary integration, which in their opinion, has been so successfully implemented in the Euro zone (Thygesen, 2002).

4.3. The New Global Exchange System and Monetary Policy of Georgia

Notwithstanding the above-said, the post-war organization of Iraq will also largely influence the international economic order. This will be a key factor that will affect economic activity of the USA.

After hostilities ended in Iraq, the UN Security Council has adopted a resolution on reversal of economic sanctions against Iraq, which fully authorizes the USA and Great Britain to attend to the post-war reorganization of the country and to manage its oil deliveries to the market (see, for example, Episheva, 2003, p. 26). It will take a definite time for this resolution to have effect on the USA.

Before the war the deliveries of Iraq to the world market attained 2 million barrels per day. While there was severe damage to the oil industry infrastructure, the Chairman of the Consultation Council at the Ministry of Oil of Iraq, Phillip Korel, considers that in the second part of 2003, oil production will surpass the pre-war level; according to some experts the benchmark will be 1.5 million barrels per day (Reutov, 2003, p. 9). However, there are more optimistic forecasts that in case of intensive investment, Iraq will be in a position to increase production up to 6 million barrels per day, ranking fourth in the world by its oil production after Saudi Arabia (8.8 million barrels), the USA (7.2 million barrels) and Russia (7.1 million barrels) (Sichinava, 2003, p. 21). With this level of production, Iraq will be able to effect market fluctuations in oil prices in the world and in a way balance out monopoly of OPEC in price-formation on the oil market.

If, with the increased deliveries of Iraqi oil, the United States allows a significant reduction in oil prices on the world market, this might cause economic downturns afterwards growing into a global economic dislocation. Development of events according to this scenario is particularly dangerous for Russia with the lion's share of its budgetary incomes accounted for by those received from the oil exports. It also presents jeopardy for Georgia, as a possible devaluation of the Russian Rouble will considerably affect its trade with Russia, which will presently find reflection in balance of payments and endanger stability of the Lari that is actually the only "bright spot" of the financial sphere.

When experts consider changes in the global exchange system acceptable (which as noted above, we think to be a bit exaggerated), this will naturally raise such questions as what will be Georgian monetary policy in the situation of "expensive" and "cheap" foreign currency and what will be positive and negative sides of maintaining the current rate of the Lari. Georgia should adapt its monetary policy while taking account of new trends forming in the world.

Given that the monetary system of Georgia is undeveloped, control of the general price level is not less important for Georgia than that of the real exchange rate of the Lari.

Separate empirical and theoretical researches show that in transition economies, institutional and structural aspects are more important for stimulating export, than currency devaluation (see, for example, Chocheli, 2003).

Some Georgian economists (as well as those of other post-communist countries) often suggest that, for stimulating economic growth and exports, devaluation of the Lari can be justified, although theoretically it has been proved that given the technical lag and by placing uncompetitive products on the market, currency devaluation would only facilitate inflation rather than production or export (Papava, 1997).

In January-May 2003, the Georgian foreign trade turnover with the EU members was USD 150 million, which compared to same indicator of the previous year is 65.6 per cent more. Of this imports account for USD 129.1 million (twice as much as during the relevant period of the previous year) (SDSG, 2003, p. 27); such growth of imports in the situation of a significant fall of the real rate of the Lari against Euro serves a good proof of the above-referred theoretical statement.

Introduction of Euro has essentially changed "world money". It has become the second major currency in the world right after "birth", constituting the third pillar of the "world money" together with the US Dollar and Yen. The exchange rates among these "three islands" of stability will become the most important prices of the world economy (Mundell, 2000).

As proceeds from the above-mentioned reality, diversification of currency reserves by the NBG is given a priority. However, while analyzing major monetary policies of Georgia in 2003 (NBG, 2002), we could outline several problems:

First, the extent of currency reserves diversification at the NBG level;

Second, the extent of diversification of deposits for commercial banks and private companies;

Third, enabling of mechanisms for option transactions (so-called "no-loss operations"), which are supposed to provide for maintenance of real value of assets on the part of both commercial banks and economic agents.

For 2002, deposits in Euro made up just 2 per cent of total deposits (Kakulia, 2003, p. 33). Should the Euro become strong while a large part of deposits is in US Dollars (83 per cent), the "losses" of economic agents will appear significant (NBG, 2003, p. 12).

Diversification of currency reserves is also essential for retaining confidence among the population, which is marginally putting at risk the remaining stability of the banking system. In January-March 2003, national currency deposits have shrunk by GEL 8.9 million and foreign currency deposits have grown by GEL

9.4 million. As against the respective period of the past year, deposits in national currency have grown by GEL 3.4 million and those in foreign currency by GEL 17 million (NBG, 2003, p. 12). As we see, expectations of economic agents, as compared to the relevant period of the last year, in 2003 are much more pessimistic. This is a result of both the undeveloped fiscal environment in the country and ongoing economic developments in the world. In particular, economic agents have decided that the US Dollar is a currency to which depreciation is not new and, like other currencies it is a reflection of the economic situation of its own country.

It should be underlined that the biggest problem for the safety of the Georgian economy is presented not by forming a "new exchange order" in the world but rather by a lack of economic policy in the country hampering regulation of the budgetary sphere and depriving Georgia of attractiveness for investment. In addition, in the absence of an optimal size public sector, Georgia runs a serious risk in its attempt to achieve economic stability and security.

And last but not least, the biggest threat to Georgia is not external shocks but the existing crisis situation inside the country (Gotsiridze, Kandelaki, 2001). This last can never be overcome unless corruption (Papava, 2000B) is deprived of its economic basis and poverty is eliminated through economic upturn (FIAC, 2003), which in turn requires carrying out serious system reforms.

References

Allen R.E., 1999. *Financial Crises and Recession in the Global Economy.* Cheltenham, Edward Elgar.

Ananova, 2002. George Soros Says Dollar May Lose a Third of its Value. www.ananova.com/business/story/sm_617615.html.

Anikin A., 2000. *History of Financial Upheavals. From John Law to Sergey Kirienko,* Moscow, "Olymp-Business". (In Russian).

Anisimov A., 2001. Financial Strategy of China. In: *Dollar Crisis.* Ed. By A. A. Nagorni. Moscow, Editor N.E. Chernishova. (In Russian).

Anušić Z., Rohatinski Ž., Šonje V. and others (ed.), 1995. *A Road to Low Inflation. Croatia 1993/1994.* Zagreb, The Government of the Republic of Croatia.

Asadov F., 2000. Oil Caravans of the 21'st Century on the Great Silk Road: what the Future has in Store for Azerbaijan and Kazakhstan. *Central Asia and the Caucasus,* No. 6.

Asatiani R., 2000. Financial Crisis and Macroeconomic Regulation of Transitional Developments in Georgia. In: *Proceedings of the Georgia Academy of Economic Sciences,* Vol. 1, Tbilisi, "Siakhle". (In Georgian).

Åslund A., 1995. *How Russia Became a Market Economy.* Washington, The Brookings Institution.

BBC, 2002. Euro Rises Near to Parity with Dollar. http://news.bbc.co.uk/1/hi/business/2067943.stm.

Bok Zi Kou, 2002. *Economy of Japan. What is it Like?* Moscow, «Izdatelstvo «Economika». (In Russian).

Britain USA, 2003. UK Economy-Key Facts, 20 May 2003. British Embassy, Washington, DC. http://www.britainusa. com/economy/xq/asp/SarticleType.1/Article ID.2904/qx/ articles show.htm#.

Chocheli V., 2003. "Syndrome of Shadow Economy": Low Tax Burden–Low Rate of Economic Growth. *Proceedings of the Georgian Academy of Sciences–Economic Series*, Vol. 11, No. 1-2. (In Georgian).

Connoly M., Melo J. de (ed.), 1994. *The Effects of Protectionism on a Small Country. The Case of Uruguay.* Washington, The World Bank.

Cottarelli C., Doyle P., 1999. *Disinflation in Transition, 1993-97.* Occasional Paper 179. Washington, IMF.

Cukrowski J., 2000. *Financing the Deficit of the State Budget by National Bank of Georgia (1996-1999).* Studies & Analyses 215. Warsaw, CASE.

Deikin A., 2001. Clinton's "New Economy" and Bush's "Proficient Plans". *SShA. Kanada. Ekonomika. Politika. Kultura*, No.10. (In Russian).

Dornbush R. (ed.), 1993. *Policymaking in the Open Economy. Concepts and Case Studies in Economic Performance.* New York, Oxford University Press.

Doronin I., Zagashvili V., Pripisnov V., 2001. World Economic Conditions in 2000–beginning of 2001. *Mirovaia ekonomika i mezhdunarodnye otnoshenia*, No. 8. (In Russian).

ECE., 2000. *Economic Survey of Europe, 2000, No. 1.* Geneva, UN.

Economist, 2002. A Cliff-hanger. *The Economist.* http://www.economist.com/ displaystory.cfm?story id= S%27%29H%28%2ARA%3B%2A%200%20T%0A

Economist, 2003. Germany's Euro Test. *The Economist.* http://www. economist.com/finance/displayStory.cfm?story id=1842183.

Elisseeff V., 2000. *The Silk Roads: Highways of Culture and Commerce.* New York, Berghahn Books.

Ellwood W., 2001. *The No-Nonsense Guide to Globalization.* Oxford, New International Publications Ltd.

Episheva L., 2003. USA Reduced Taxes by 350 billion. *Macro Micro Economics*, No. 5. (In Georgian).

FIAC, 2003. Economic Development and Poverty Reduction Program of Georgia. http://www.fiac.ge/Documents/EDPRP%20_ENG_%20FINAL.pdf.

Fisher S., Sakhai R., 1997. Stabilization and Growth in Transitional Economies: First Lessons. *Voprosy ekonomiki*, No. 5. (In Russian).

Foltz R.C., 1999. *Religions of the Silk Rod: Overland Trade and Cultural Exchange from Antiquity to the Fifteenth Century.* New York, St. Martin's Press.

Gachechiladze R., 1995. *The New Georgia. Space, Society, Politics.* London, UCL Press.

Gaidar E., 1997. *Anomaly of Economic Growth.* Moscow, Eurasia. (In Russian).

Gamsakhurdia G., 1997. *Role of Finance in Georgian Transitional Economy.* Tbilisi, "Meridiani". (In Georgian).

Gates B., 1999. *Business @ the Speed of Thought.* New York, Warner Books Inc.

Gazeta, 2003. USA Businessmen Rescue Dollar from Asia. http://www.gazeta.ru/2003/06/17/kz_m89155.shtml.

Gegeshidze A.M., 1999A. The South Caucasus: Getting Close to Europe? *Marco Polo Magazine*, No. 1.

Gegeshidze A.M., 1999B. Once Again on the Great Silk Road. *Central Asia and the Caucasus*, No. 3. (In Russian).

Gelbras V., Kuznetsova V., 2001. Chinese People's Republic. *Mirovaia ekonomka i mezhdunarodnye otnoshenia*, No. 8. (In Russian).

Ghosh A.R., Gulde A.-M., Ostry J.D., Wolf H., 1996. *Does the Exchange Rate Regime Matter for Inflation and Growth?* Washington, IMF.

Gold, 2001. Gold Important in Maintaining Public Confidence Security of Reserves a Key Factor. http://www.gold.org/pr_archive/html/191101.html

Gotsiridze R., Kandelaki O., 2001. Georgia: Halfway Reforms as a Factor of the Economic Crisis. *Central Asia and the Caucasus,* No. 6.

Gurgenidze L., Lobzhanidze M., Onoprishvili D., 1994. Georgia: From Planning to Hyperinflation. *Communist Economies & Economic Transformation,* Vol. 6, No. 2.

IMF, 2001A. *International Financial Statistics, 2001* (October). Washington, IMF.

IMF, 2001B. *The Information Technology Revolution. World Economic Outlook, 2001* (October). Washington, IMF.

IMF, 2003. *SDR Valuation, October 2003.* http://www.imf.org/external/np/tre/sdr/basket.htm.

Iša J., 2002. Eurozone and World Economy. *BEATEC,* Vol. X, No. 2.

Jochem A., 1999. Monetary Stabilization in Countries in Transition. *International Advances in Economic Research,* Vol., 5, No. 1.

Kakulia M., 2001A. Substance and Forms of Modern Currency Crises. *Obschestvo i ekonomika,* No. 5. (In Russian).

Kakulia M., 2001B. *Problems of Currency System Development in Georgia.* Tbilisi, SESPSKI. (In Georgian).

Kakulia M., 2003. Euro on the Georgian Currency Market: is the US Dollar Giving up its Positions? *Macro Micro Economics,* No. 4. (In Georgian).

Kakulia M., Aslamazishvili N., 2000. *Dollarization in Georgia: Scale, Factors, Ways of Overcoming.* Tbilisi, Georgia Academy of Sciences P. Gugushvili Institute of Economics. (In Georgian).

Kakulia R., 1998. The Monetary System Reform in Georgia. *Obschestvo i ekonomika,* No. 2. (In Russian).

Kelly K., 1998. *New Rules for the New Economy. 10 Ways the Network Economy is Changing Everything.* London, Fourth Estate.

Khazin M., Grigoriev O., 2001. Scenario of the Dollar Crisis in the Near-Term Outlook. In: *Dollar Crisis.* Ed. By A. A. Nagorni. Moscow, Editor N.E. Chernishova. (In Russian).

Kistauri L., 2000. Stimulating Economic Growth by Increased Money Supply: Myth and Reality. *Banki*, No. 1. (In Georgian).

Klaus V., 1997. Promoting Financial Stability in the Transition Economies of Central and Eastern Europe. In: *Maintaining Financial Stability in a Global Economy.* A Symposium Sponsored by The Federal Reserve of Kansas City. Jacson Hole. Wyoming, August 28-30, 1997.

Kornai J., 1993. Transformational Recession: A General Phenomenon Examined Through the Example of Hungary's Development. *Economic Appliqué*, Vol. 46, Vo. 2.

Kovzanadze I., 2002. System Banking Crises under the Conditions of Financial Globalization. *Voprosy ekonomiki*, No. 8. (In Russian).

Kovzanadze I., 2003. *Systemic Banking Crises in the Conditions of Financial Globalization.* Tbilisi, Tbilisi University Press. (In Russian).

Krasavina L.N. (ed.), 2000. *Inflation and the Anti-Inflationary Policy in Russia.* Moscow, "Finance and Statistics". (In Russian).

Lavigne M., 1995. *The Economics of Transition. From Socialist Economy to Market Economy.* New York, St. Martin's Press.

Liu X., 1998. *The Silk Road: Overland Trade and Cultural Interactions in Eurasia.* Washington, American Historical Association.

Managadze I., 2002. Regulation of Inflation as a Key Problem of Macroeconomic Stabilization. *Macro-Micro Economics*, No. 7/8. (In Georgian).

Martirosian A., 2000. The Great Silk Road Restored. *Central Asia and the Caucasus*, No. 6.

Melo M. de, Denizer C., Gelb A., 1997. From Plan to Market: Patterns of Transition. In: *Macroeconomic Stabilization in Transition Economies.* Ed. by M. I. Blejer, M. Škreb. Cambridge, Cambridge University Press.

Meskhia I., 2000. Modern Problems of Georgia's Financial and Economic Security. In: *Georgia's Financial and Economic Problems in the Transitional Period.* Vol. 4, Tbilisi, FSKI. (In Georgian).

Meskhia Y., Iashvili R., 1998. Monetary Policy in Georgia. *Voprosy ekonomiki,* No. 9. (In Russian).

Metreveli R., 1995. *Georgia.* Nashville, Publisher's International.

Mikhailovich D., 2003. Euro Still Has Growth Potential. *Comerssant,* No.89, 26 May. (In Russian).

Mundell, R. A., 2000. Reconsideration of the Twentieth Century. *The American Economic Review,* Vol. 90, No. 3.

Nariai O., 2002. *The Modern Japanese Economy.* About Japan Series 2. Tokyo, The Foreign Press Center.

NBG, 2002. Decree of the Parliament of Georgia: "On Main Trends of the 2003 Monetary Policy of Georgia". (In Georgian). http://www.nbg.gov.ge/geo/savaluto_politika/index_4.html

NBG, 2003. *Monetary and Bank Statistics Bulletin, No. 1.* Tbilisi, The NBG. (In Georgian).

Papava V., 1991. *Some Problems of the Economic Independence of Georgia and the Transition to the Market Economy.* Tbilisi, "Metsniereba".

Papava V., 1995. The Georgian Economy: Problems of Reform. *Eurasian Studies,* Vol., 2, No. 2.

Papava V., 1996. The Georgian Economy: From "Shock Therapy" to "Social Promotion". *Communist Economies & Economic Transformation,* Vol. 8, No. 8.

Papava V., 1997. Monetary Policy in Georgia: Tough or Liberal? *Macro Micro Economics,* December. (In Georgian).

Papava V., 1998. Toward the Progress of Reform and Prospects of Economic Growth. *Obscestvo i ekonomika*, No. 2. (In Russian).

Papava V., 1999. The Georgian Economy: Main Directions and Initial Results of Reforms. In: *Systemic Change in Post-Communist Economies*. Selected Papers from the Fifth World Congress of Central and East European Studies, Warsaw, 1995. Ed. by P. G. Hare. London, Macmillan Press.

Papava V., 2000A. *Inflationary Impact on Economic Growth*. Banki, No. 1. (In Georgian).

Papava V., 2000B. Economic Approach to the Restriction of Corruption in Georgia. *Georgian Economic Trends*, No. 3-4.

Papava V., 2002A. *Leszek Balcerowicz and Georgia*. Tbilisi, GFSIS, 2002.

Papava V., 2002B. On the Formation of Economic System in the Southern Caucasus. *Obscestvo i ekonomika*, No. 1. (In Russian).

Papava V., 2002C. On the Special Features of Georgia's International Economic Function. *Central Asia and the Caucasus*, No. 2.

Papava V., 2002D. On the Possibilities and Prospects for the Formation of an Economic System in the Southern Caucasus. In: *Central Asia and South Caucasus Affairs: 2002*. Ed. by. B. Rumer and Lau S.Y. Tokyo, The Sasakawa Peace Foundation.

Papava V., 2002E. Necroeconomics–the Theory of Post-Communist Transformation of an Economy. *International Journal of Social Economics*, Vol. 29, No. 9-10.

Papava V., Beridze T., 1994. Problems of Reforming Georgia's Economy. *Rossijski' ekonomiceski' zhurnal*, No. 3. (In Russian).

Papava V., Beridze T., 1998. Economic Reforms in Georgia. *Rossijski' ekonomiceski' zhurnal*, No. 1. (In Russian).

Papava V., Chikovani E. (ed.), 1997. Georgia: Economic and Social Challenges of the Transition. *Problems of Economic Transition*, Vol. 40, No. 7/8.

Papava V., Chocheli V., 2002. Possibility of a Global Economic Crisis and the Strategy of Georgia. *Georgian Economic Trends*, 2002 No. 1.

Papava V., Gogatadze N., 1998. Prospects for Foreign Investments and Strategic Economic Partnership in the Caucasus. *Problems of Economic Transition*, Vol. 41, No. 5.

Patrytski S., 2000. Inflation and Social Conflicts. In: *Economics and Politics in Transitional Society: Crisis of Interrelationships.* Ed. by L. I. Nikovskaia. Moscow, Editorial URSS. (In Russian).

Pravda, 1999. Dollar and Euro Game in Full Swing. http://english.pravda.ru/ main/18/89/356/10110 .html.

Reutov A., 2003. Iraq is Deprived of the Last. The USA are Changing Sanctions on oil. *Commerssant*, No. 92, May 29. (In Russian).

Rondeli A., 1999. TRACECA: a Tool for Regional Cooperation in the Caucasus. *Marco Polo Magazine*, No. 1.

Rondeli A., 2001. The Choice of Independent Georgia. In: *The Security of the Caspian Sea Region.* Ed. by G. Chufrin. New York, Oxford University Press.

Rondeli A., 2003. *Small States in the International System.* Tbilisi, "Metsniereba". (In Georgian).

Rubtsov B., 2001. World Financial Markets. *Mirovaia ekonomika i mezhdunarodnye otnoshenia*, No. 8.

Rumer B., 2000. Economic Crisis and Growing Intraregional Tensions. In: *Central Asia and the New Global Economy.* Ed. by B. Rumer. Armonk, M.E.Sharpe.

Schmieding H., 1993. From Plan to Market: On the Nature of the Transformational Crises. *Weltwirtschaftliches Archiw*, Vol. 129, No. 2.

SDSG, 2002. *Social and Economic Situation in Georgia. Georgian Statistical Review 2002.* Tbilisi, State Department of Statistics of Georgia. (In Georgian).

SDSG, 2003. *Social and Economic Situation in Georgia. Georgian Statistical Review, January-May 2003.* Tbilisi, State Department of Statistics of Georgia. (In Georgian).

Shevardnadze E., 1999. *Great Silk Route. TRACECA-PETrA. Transport Corridor Europe-Caucasus-Asia. The Eurasian Common Market. Political and Economic Aspects.* Tbilisi, Georgian Transport System Ltd.

Sichinava S., 2003. Black Oil–Red Line of World Interests. *Macro Micro Economics,* No.1. (In Georgian).

Stiglitz J.E., 2002. *Globalization and its Discontents.* New York, W.W.Norton & Company.

Stroev E.S., Bliakhman L.S., Krotov M.I., 1999. *Russia and Eurasia at the Crossroads. Experience and Problems of Economic Reforms in the Commonwealth of Independent States.* Berlin, Springer.

Sušjan A., Lah M., 1997. Inflation in the Transition Economies: the Post-Keynesian View. *Review of Political Economy,* Vol. 9, No. 4.

Tavlas J.S., 2001. International Use of Currencies. In: *Advanced Macroeconomic and Financial Management,* Vol. 1. Vienna, IMF Institute.

Thygesen N., 2002. The Path to the Euro for Enlargement Countries. http://www.europarl.eu.int/comparl/econ/pdf/emu/speeches/20020521/thygesen.pdf.

USA Today, 2003. Euro Rises to Record Level Against the US Dollar. http://www.usatoday.com/money/markets/2003-05-27-euro_x.htm

Wang J.-Y., 1998. From Coupon to Lari: Hyperinflation and Stabilization in Georgia. *Caucasica. The Journal of Caucasian Studies,* Vol. 1.

Wellisz S., 1996. *Georgia: A Brief Survey of Macroeconomic Problems and Policies.* Studies & Analyses 87. Warsaw, CASE.

Wellisz S., 1997. Inflation and Stabilization in Poland, 1990-1995. In: *Macroeconomic Stabilization in Transition Economies.* Ed. by M. I. Blejer, M. Škreb. Cambridge, Cambridge University Press.

Zak P.J. (ed.), 1999. *Currency Crises, Monetary Union and the Conduct of Monetary Policy. A Debate Among Leading Economists.* Cheltenham, Edward Elgar.

Zhukow S., 2000. Adapting to Globalization. In: *Central Asia and the New Global Economy.* Ed. by B. Rumer. Armonk, M.E.Sharpe.

Zhyrny A., Yarochinskiy M., 1997. *Monetary Policy and Inflation in Georgia in 1996 to 1998.* Studies and Analysis, No. 114. (In Russian).

Zukowski R., 1996. Transformation Crisis in Post-Socialist Countries: Patterns and Causes. *International Journal of Social Economics*, Vol. 23, No.10/11.

Zvania Z., 1998. Georgia and the New Geopolitical Function of the Caucasus. *Caucasica: The Journal of Caucasian Studies*, No. 2.